# Who Is Rita Moreno?

by G. M. Taboas Zayas

illustrated by Tim Foley

Penguin Workshop

For my Ma, Adaljisa—GMTZ

PENGUIN WORKSHOP
An imprint of Penguin Random House LLC
1745 Broadway, New York, NY 10019
penguinrandomhouse.com

Library of Congress Cataloging-in-Publication Data is available.

First published in the United States of America by Penguin Workshop, 2026

Manufactured in the United States of America
CJKW

ISBN 9780593891063 (paperback)
10 9 8 7 6 5 4 3 2 1

ISBN 9780593891056 (library binding)
10 9 8 7 6 5 4 3 2 1

The authorized representative in the EU for product safety and compliance is Penguin Random House Ireland, Morrison Chambers, 32 Nassau Street, Dublin D02 YH68, Ireland, https://eu-contact.penguin.ie.

# Contents

ST SID
OSCAR

# Who Is Rita Moreno?

During the Academy Awards ceremony on April 9, 1962, a talented Puerto Rican actress named Rita Moreno sat and waited with her friends. She'd been nominated for the award of best supporting actress for her role as Anita in the movie *West Side Story*. The Academy Awards celebrates people in the film industry for their outstanding work.

Rita had flown all the way to Los Angeles, California, from the Philippines, where she was working on a film called *Cry of Battle*. She was so excited just to be attending the awards ceremony that she didn't even have a speech prepared.

They announced the first few winners: Maximilian Schell won best actor for *Judgment at Nuremberg*, George Chakiris won best supporting actor for *West Side Story*, then Sophia Loren won best actress for *Two Women*.

Finally, it was time to announce who won best supporting actress. Rock Hudson, an American actor, was presenting the award. He read out the names of the other nominated actors: Judy Garland, Fay Bainter, Lotte Lenya, and

Una Merkel, all talented and famous women—but Rita was the only Puerto Rican person and the only woman of color nominated for the award. When Rock Hudson announced Rita as the winner, she was speechless! She was the first Puerto Rican woman to win an Academy Award! When she walked to the stage to accept her award, Rita didn't quite know what to say.

She'd been performing since she was a little girl, dancing and acting in front of her family and friends, auditioning and acting in movies for the chance to be a star. On that stage, Rita felt like her dream was finally coming true.

"I can't believe it!" she said, grinning from ear to ear.

That same night back in New York City, where Rita lived for most of her childhood, people throughout the city celebrated her win. Puerto Ricans in El Barrio—meaning "neighborhood" or "district" in Spanish—also known as Spanish Harlem because of the large Hispanic and Latin communities who lived there, cried out, "She won! She won!" From their windows and out on the streets they yelled: "She *did* it!"

# CHAPTER 1
# Life Before the Big Change

Rita Moreno, whose birth name is Rosita Dolores Alverio, was born on December 11, 1931, in Humacao, Puerto Rico. She lived the first five years of her life in Juncos, at the edge of El Yunque (say: JUN-ke), a national forest on the east end of the island, with her family. Her mother was named Rosa Maria Alverio and her father, Paco José Alverio. Rosita had a baby brother called Francisco, and they all lived in a pink house surrounded by hibiscus flowers. Rosita called all the houses in her village "ice cream" houses because of their pretty bright colors.

Her childhood was spent surrounded by her family, making sailboats out of banana leaves,

racing small frogs called coquis (say: ko-KEES), and playing with her pet Puchito, a baby chick who followed her everywhere. Rita was a smart

child, able to guess what plants Rosa was holding just by smell, like recao (say: reh-KA-o), which is also known as culantro.

## El Yunque

Puerto Rico

El Yunque National Forest is a tropical rainforest in the northeastern part of Puerto Rico, close to the Río Grande region. It became a national forest in 1906. And while it is the only tropical rainforest in the United States National Forest System, it is also the most diverse for having such a wide variety of plant and animal life. These include Tabonuco Forest, Palo Colorado Forest, Sierra-Palm Forest, and the Dwarf Forest, the red fruit bat, the Puerto Rican boa, the guaragüao hawk, the famous coqui frog, and the Puerto Rican Amazon parrot.

It rains year-round in El Yunque, where there are natural rivers and waterfalls named La Coca and La Mina.

The native Taíno (say: tah-ee-noh) people named the rainforest Yuke, which means "white earth," because of the clouds that gather at the peak. Some believe that the name comes from Yúcahu (say: ju-ka-u), who was the deity of fertility to the Taínos.

Rosita's mother always made sure Rosita and Francisco were dressed nicely, especially when they went to Catholic church. Rosita sometimes thought that her mother only liked to dress her up so she could show off to everyone how pretty and smart Rosita was.

In 1935, when Rosita was four years old, her mother moved from Puerto Rico to New York City, or as Rosita called it, "the big America." Rosa was gone for two months, working hard to make a new life for herself and Rosita. Many

Puerto Ricans moved to the United States for the same reason, to earn enough to take care of their families and hopefully bring them to America to live with them. Since the United States invaded the island in 1898, later declaring Puerto Ricans to be American citizens, they were allowed to move freely to the United States.

Rosa came back to Puerto Rico just in time for Christmas, with many presents for Rosita and her little brother. For Rosita, it was the best Christmas she ever had. She did not know it would be her last Christmas in Juncos.

## CHAPTER 2
## The Big Change

Right after Christmas, in 1936, Rosa and Rosita boarded the SS *Carabobo* and sailed for five days. On its way to New York City, the ship nearly sank when it sailed through a hurricane!

Rosa only took Rosita, leaving her husband and Francisco behind. Rosita begged her to take Francisco with her, and Rosa promised she would come back when he was older, but Rosita never saw her younger brother again. For Rosita, now five years old, this was the "big change."

Arriving in New York City, Rosa and Rosita moved into a four-room apartment in the Bronx with twelve other people. Rosita compared the change from Puerto Rico to the United States to the film *The Wizard of Oz*, but in reverse: from bright, beautiful colors to gray and grimy.

Life was not easy in New York. On her first night, Rosita was bitten by bedbugs and the cold weather made her terribly sick. The radiator in the building she lived in would turn off at times, making it an even colder place to live and sleep. And Rosita and her mother were sometimes treated cruelly. Puerto Ricans, despite being American citizens, were not considered to be true Americans, since Puerto Rico was a territory ruled by the United States. They were treated like outsiders, like many other people who immigrated to New York in search of new opportunities. Rosita had a difficult time in school because she did not speak English yet. She decided to practice English so she could be fluent—able to speak a different language as easily as possible.

Rosa worked hard to save as much money as she could so that they could move to a new apartment. She worked in factories and cleaned houses. Rosita helped sell tissue-paper flowers that Rosa made. When they had enough, they moved to Washington Heights. It was after the move to their new home that someone saw Rosita dancing in front of Rosa's friends and suggested that Rosita take dance lessons.

Rosa enrolled Rosita, now six years old, in the dance studio of Paco Cansino, a Spanish dancer who was also the uncle of Rita Hayworth, a famous American actress. Rita Hayworth would become Rosita's greatest inspiration and role model. Paco taught Rosita everything he knew, and when she turned nine, he arranged for her to perform live for the first time in a Greenwich Village club.

Dressed in a ruffled skirt and wearing makeup and flowers in her hair, Rosita felt like she had become a different person. As she danced in front of the crowd, her love of performing blossomed.

## Rita Hayworth (1918–1987)

Born Margarita Carmen Cansino in Brooklyn, New York, Rita Hayworth was an American film actress who appeared in over sixty films.

Rita grew up performing with her parents, Spanish dancer Eduardo Cansino and American

Volga Hayworth, in dance shows and in short films like *La Fiesta* in 1926. She was discovered by Fox Studios when she was sixteen, and then got a new contract working for Columbia Pictures. She starred in *Only Angels Have Wings* with British actor Cary Grant, *Cover Girl*, and *Tonight and Every Night*, becoming more popular with every movie she worked in. Rita Hayworth's most famous film was *Gilda* in 1946, which was a film noir, a movie term for crime drama. She even became a real-life princess when she married Prince Aly Khan in 1949!

Rita continued to work with Hollywood legends including Orson Welles and Fred Astaire, until her final film, *The Wrath of God*, in 1972.

# CHAPTER 3
# First Film

Since her first performance in that club, Rosita was determined to do anything to be on the stage once again. She did impressions of Carmen Miranda, a Portuguese Brazilian performer who was known for singing and dancing while wearing a headdress that held grapes, bananas, and other fruit. Rosita danced at weddings and bar mitzvahs. Her mother sewed dresses for her and built a small headdress with plastic fruit. After the US entered World War II

Carmen Miranda

in 1941, Rosita performed for soldiers in New York City before they went to war. She sang songs like "O Tique-Taque do Meu Coração," which means "Tic-Tac of My Heart."

Rosita was booked to sing in clubs and speak in radio productions, where people performed plays, musicals, and operas broadcast over the radio. She did voice acting for *The Ave Maria Hour*, stories about the lives of saints and gospels for radio audiences listening at home.

At this time, some movies had the voices of the actors overdubbed from English to Spanish for Spanish-speaking audiences. Rosita worked in a recording studio to create some of the Spanish audio. Doing this work made Rosita want to be

on the big screen. She longed to be the leading lady of a movie!

Rosa was supportive of Rosita's goals, especially since it helped pay the bills. She pushed Rosita to do more and more, even though she was still in school. Rosita was happy to do it because she loved the work and being in the spotlight.

At thirteen years old, in 1945, Rosita landed her first part on a Broadway show called *Skydrift*. The show closed very shortly after because of poor reviews, but the experience pushed Rosita to try even harder to build her career. She decided to drop out of school to focus on becoming an actress.

Rosa eventually married Edward Moreno, who worked in the same Spanish radio station Rosita did, and they all moved into a small house in Valley Stream, a small town on Long Island, New York.

Rosa gave birth to Rosita's second younger brother, Denis Moreno, whom she adored. But she thought Edward was very overbearing, and her mother soon divorced him. Rosita began traveling back and forth from her home on Long Island to nightclubs in the city, carrying an old suitcase with all her dresses and makeup.

Sometimes her trips were almost six hours long by buses and trains!

But Rosita auditioned every chance she could. She rode trains and buses to readings, hoping to be cast in a movie role. She now called herself Rosita Moreno, using her stepfather's last name since it was easier to pronounce than Alverio.

Part of auditioning for movies meant Rosita also needed to find an agent. A talent agent manages the career of an actor, helps find them work, and negotiates contracts for them. Rosita would look for their names in magazines and call them to make appointments to meet them. When she was fifteen, Rosita found an agent who wanted to work with her. He invited her to his home. Rosita was uncomfortable with how the man looked at her. After he touched her without her permission, she ran from the house.

In 1950, when Rosita was eighteen years old, she auditioned for her first movie role in *So Young, So Bad*, which told the story of three young women who lived in prison. And Rosita got the part! In the movie, she played Dolores Guerrero, a sweet, lonely girl who played the guitar. The movie was filmed in New York and Connecticut.

*So Young, So Bad* is the only film where Rosita has been credited as Rosita Moreno.

While the movie was not very popular after it came out, Rosita was proud of her work in it. The movie was just the start of much bigger things.

# CHAPTER 4
# Hollywood!

Louis B. Mayer

One day, while at a dance recital, a talent agent noticed Rosita. He wanted her to meet Louis B. Mayer, who was a film producer—someone who helped make movies by choosing scripts, hiring directors, and also financing the productions. Mr. Mayer had cofounded Metro-Goldwyn-Mayer (MGM), a film studio that made movies like *The Wizard of Oz* and *Gone with the Wind.*

The meeting with Mr. Mayer happened after Rosita finished working on *So Young, So Bad* in

1950. She and her mother worked hard to make her look as beautiful as possible. Rosita wanted to look like Elizabeth Taylor, a famous actress who acted in films like *Lassie Come Home*, *Little Women*, and many more. Rosita fixed her hair and put on makeup to make her dark skin look a little lighter. When she looked in the mirror, she did not recognize herself. She no longer looked like a girl who was born and raised in Puerto Rico.

With her mother, Rosita met Louis B. Mayer in the Waldorf Astoria Hotel. As soon as she met Mr. Mayer, he said, "She looks like a Spanish Elizabeth Taylor!" Then he immediately offered her a seven-year contract to work at MGM Studios.

## The Golden Age of Hollywood (1920s–1960s)

The Golden Age of Hollywood was a period where filmmaking began to move away from silent movies because they were limited to short scenes with wide angles. It was a time when filmmakers experimented and tested new ways to produce films. They created large sets, changed the angles of the camera, and introduced sound into their films. They later introduced color, too. (Before the 1930s, almost all films had been black and white. And even up until the 1950s, color film was not very common.)

The companies that had the biggest influence during the Golden Age were MGM, Twentieth Century–Fox, Paramount, RKO, and Warner Bros., who released well-known movies such as *King Kong*, *The Wizard of Oz*, *Singin' in the Rain*, and many more. Each company had superstar actors such as

Humphrey Bogart, Cary Grant, Grace Kelly, Marilyn Monroe, and Rita Hayworth, who worked exclusively for them. During this time, directors, writers, and actors were all employees of the major studios.

For Rosita, her life changed so quickly in that moment that it became a blur. In less than six months, she and her family quickly sold the house in New York and moved to Culver City, California. Eddie, Rosa's husband, joined the army and was sent to Japan, and they divorced soon after.

Rosita was paid two hundred dollars a week, and she bought a car and taught herself how to drive. No more buses and trains for her!

During her first week at MGM Studios, she met several famous actors such as Ava Gardner, Clark Gable, and many other stars—people she had only seen on the big screen! But she wasn't treated the same. She guessed it was because she was Puerto Rican, but Rosita knew she belonged there as much as anyone else.

One day, she was told she needed to meet a famous casting agent named Bill Grady in his office. She was terrified they were going to fire her before she even started working in a movie.

Instead, Bill looked at her and said, "Your name has to go. Too Italian." He started suggesting different names for her such as Ruby Fontino, Marcy Miranda, even Orchid Montenegro, until he finally decided on Rita, after Rita Hayworth. Rosita felt it was a sign of great things, being named after someone she idolized who was also related to her former Spanish dance teacher, Paco. Rosita from Juncos, Puerto Rico, was no more.

“Rita Moreno,” Bill said. “That’s who you are and that’s who you’ll be.”

Rita worked on musicals such as *The Toast of New Orleans*, *Pagan Love Song*, and more. In all of them, she was always a supportive character and had to play a stereotypical ethnic (meaning non-white) character. She was cast in roles to play Tahitians, Hawaiians, or Indigenous people. She tried to get the lead roles, even tried to make her skin look lighter with makeup, but Rita continued to be hired for the same type of character over and over again. Her manager of that time said that directors and producers didn't even want to consider her. They had already decided that she wasn't meant to play a lead role without even giving her a chance.

But in 1952, a famous dancer and actor named Gene Kelly picked Rita to play Zelda Zanders for a musical named *Singin' in the Rain*. For the first time since Rita was hired at MGM, she did not play an "ethnic" girl but a famous silent-film actress!

Gene asked her to cut her hair short for the role, and while Rita was always happy to do what needed to be done for her job, this was a line she would not cross. “Cutting hair is not the custom in Puerto Rico,” she told Gene. “Girls and women never cut their hair; it is a point of feminine pride.”

Luckily, they settled with her wearing a red wig. Rita loved working on *Singin’ in the Rain* and was ecstatic and hopeful that she wouldn’t have to act as an “ethnic girl” ever again.

But after she worked on the musical with Gene Kelly, roles for Rita stopped coming in. She wasn’t getting called for anything. When Rita couldn't wait any longer, she went straight to Bill Grady, who told her she was fired from MGM Studios.

Her last words to Bill were simply, "Thank you."

She was back to square one. But Rita refused to let that stop her. Rosa started working again to help pay bills, sewing and cooking in restaurants, and Rita started to audition again. She would take anything, and do anything, to be a star.

# CHAPTER 5
# *Life* Magazine and Marlon Brando

In 1954, an editor at *Life* magazine picked Rita to be on the cover of their next issue. The cover caught the attention of Darryl F. Zanuck, a film producer, who signed her for a new seven-year contract with Twentieth Century–Fox, another film studio in Hollywood. She was twenty-five years old and was cast as Tuptim in the musical *The King and I*, a story about a teacher who taught the children of King Mongkut of Siam in the 1860s.

She was bored playing Tuptim, who was a sad girl in a forbidden romance with a prince, and Rita was frustrated that she was cast as a minor character yet again.

Rita played a Cheyenne Indian in *The Yellow Tomahawk* and a Mohican girl in *The Deerslayer*. Hollywood did not know what to do with someone like Rita Moreno. Even though she could sing, dance, and act, she was only hired to play similar characters in every film. But Rita needed the money, and she was convinced that someday someone would discover her real talent as an actress.

She was frustrated that people in the movie industry wanted her to use an accent to make her sound and look more like she was from a particular cultural group. Rita began to feel uncomfortable with her own heritage. She felt it was holding her back from better opportunities.

Now, when she acted in those roles, no matter what background the character had, she started using the same accent over and over again. It didn't matter who she played, no one noticed, or cared, how she spoke.

Marlon Brando

Around that time, Rita met Marlon Brando on the set of *Désirée*. Marlon was a handsome, talented actor who actually noticed Rita from the very magazine cover that got her signed with Twentieth Century–Fox. They immediately fell in love, but their relationship was difficult. Marlon was rude to the people he worked with. And he was sometimes rude to Rita. They tried to make each other jealous. And Rita even once

dated Elvis Presley to get Marlon's attention—and it worked!

The drama of this relationship hurt Rita very much, and she had a difficult time with her physical and mental health. A doctor even suggested to her that the only way to heal was to never see Marlon again. At one point, Rita became pregnant with Marlon's child, but due to health complications, Rita lost her baby.

Her work as an actress wasn't getting any easier, either. In 1955, she played Ula, the daughter of a chief in California. In her last scene, Ula dies by falling off a cliff and into the sea. Rita didn't know the water was filled with jellyfish, and they were stinging her while she pretended to be dead.

The director, frustrated with Rita as she tried

to explain that she was in pain, said in front of everyone, “Shut up and do as I say!” He didn’t see her as Rita, an actress, but as an object in his movie. This was not the first time Rita was treated poorly while working. But she always did her best to defend herself and prove that she deserved to be there just as much as everyone else.

## CHAPTER 6
## *West Side Story* and the Academy Awards

In 1961, Rita was cast in the movie adaptation of the Broadway musical *West Side Story*. This was a well-known musical that had been directed by Jerome Robbins with music written by Leonard Bernstein and Stephen Sondheim.

To get the role, Rita had to audition for three days. She needed to prove to the producers and the director that she could sing, dance, and act. Her perseverance and determination helped her win the role of Anita.

Even though half the characters in the story were Puerto Rican, Rita was one of the only Puerto Ricans in the movie. And she was forced to put on makeup, like the rest of the cast, to look more "brown." For Rita, it was insulting to see her culture painted into one single type and only one color. Puerto Ricans are a variety of different complexions because of their ancestors—from white to brown to Black.

## *West Side Story*

*West Side Story* was inspired by William Shakespeare's *Romeo and Juliet*, a tragic tale of two people who fall in love while their families are at war. For *West Side Story*, the story was set in the Upper West Side of New York City, and the rivals were teen gang members: the Puerto Rican Sharks and the white American Jets.

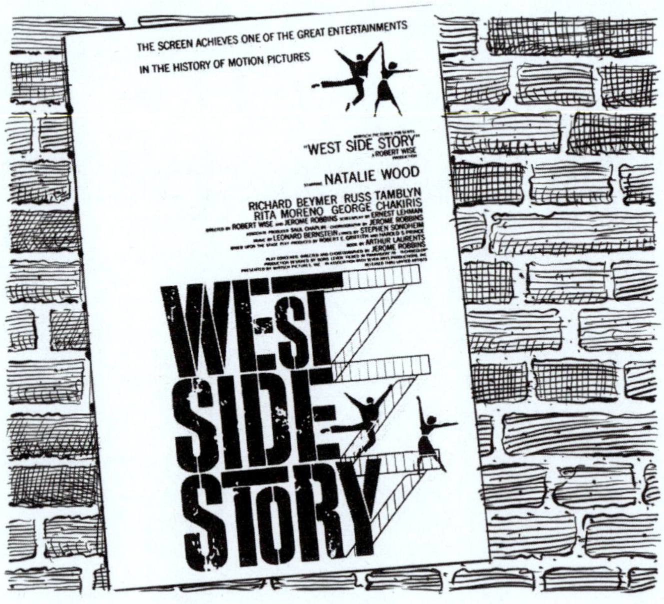

The story was written by Arthur Laurents, with lyrics by Stephen Sondheim and music by Leonard Bernstein. The musical opened on September 26, 1957, at the Winter Garden Theatre. It was nominated for six Tony Awards and won for Best Choreography and Scenic Design. The 1961 movie adaptation won ten Academy Awards, including Best Picture, and a Grammy for best soundtrack.

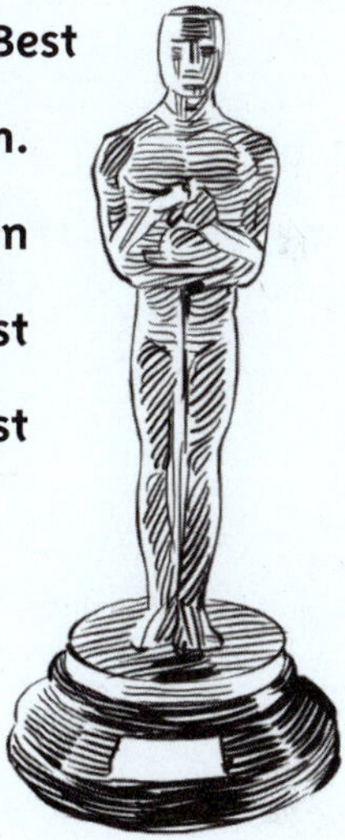

*West Side Story* returned to Broadway four more times. Steven Spielberg adapted the movie again in 2021, and it was then nominated for several awards, including Best Picture. Ariana DeBose won the Academy Award for best supporting actress.

But Rita did love playing Anita—a character who said what was on her mind and who defended herself. Rita admired how the character of Anita knew right from wrong, and Rita could connect with her anger at being treated poorly for being different. But she felt uncomfortable about Anita's dislike of Puerto Rico. Rita was proud of where she was from.

The role was also difficult for her physical health. The choreography—the dance routines—was hard on her knees even though she was still in her twenties. And she was exhausted because she was filming two movies at one time. Not only was she working on *West Side Story*, but she was also acting in another film called *Summer and Smoke*,

Rita and her costar filming *Summer and Smoke*

a movie based on a play written by Tennessee Williams. But where Anita was angry and exciting, her role as Rosa Zacharias in *Summer and Smoke* was the same stereotypical Latina, a young woman who always needed a man to protect her.

On February 26, 1962, while Rita was working in the Philippines on a movie called *Cry of Battle*, she received a telegram—a message sent by telegraph wires and then printed out—from her agent saying that she had been nominated for an Academy Award, also called an Oscar, as best supporting actress for *West Side Story*.

It did not occur to Rita that she would ever be nominated for an Oscar. She was only thirty years old. The first Latin actor who ever won an Oscar was José Ferrer, a Puerto Rican who won best actor for the 1950 film *Cyrano de Bergerac*. The second one to win was Anthony Quinn, a Mexican actor who won best supporting actor in 1952 for *Viva Zapata!* and best actor in 1957 for *Wild Is the Wind*.

Rita flew to Los Angeles and on April 9 went to the Academy Awards ceremony with her friend and *West Side Story* costar George Chakiris. She was so happy to attend that she didn't care if she won or lost.

But when they called her name as the winner for best supporting actress, she was so surprised and speechless that when she walked up to the stage to accept her award, she simply said, "I can't believe it . . . I leave you with that!" Many people said that it was one of the shortest acceptance speeches ever said in Academy Awards history.

The support of her friends, her family, and the Latin and Hispanic community far outshone the award. And on the day she flew back to the Philippines to continue her work on the film, all the Filipinos working with her sang and congratulated her. "*Mabuhay*, Rita! Victory, Rita!"

# CHAPTER 7
# Rita's Activism

After winning the Oscar, Rita began to take an interest in political activism, where a group of people fight for a cause they think needs to change or improve. Rita discovered she was capable of helping others and she could raise awareness on issues she believed in. Because she was popular, seen on television, and listened to, she could use her influence and her fame to give a voice to causes that she believed in.

On August 28, 1963, Rita and many other celebrities, like Bob Dylan, Sammy Davis Jr., and James Garner, traveled to Washington, DC, to participate in the March on Washington for Jobs and Freedom. Over two hundred and

fifty thousand people marched to the nation's capital that day. For Rita, the air was filled with energy and hope.

At the Lincoln Memorial, Rita sat close to the podium and listened to speeches by John Lewis, who was a Georgia state representative and who spoke for racial equality, meaning people of all races and ethnicities are treated the same and given the same opportunities in life, and Dr. Martin Luther King Jr. His "I Have a Dream" speech inspired Rita to dream of an America with equal opportunity, where people would never be judged by how they looked or where they came from but by who they were.

Dr. Martin Luther King Jr.

The March on Washington for Jobs and Freedom inspired Rita to become a lifelong activist. She began to learn more about politics and what was going on in the world and how she could help. She participated in a protest to “ban the bomb.” Scientists discovered that small pieces of strontium-90, a radioactive chemical deposit from atomic tests, had been landing on fields containing dairy cows. The chemical was getting into the milk sold in grocery stores. If it wasn’t banned, drinking milk would be dangerous.

Rita also saw protests as a way to push against the unfair treatment of women. She would spend the rest of her life fighting for the rights of women to protect their bodies and to end discrimination.

Rita was also able to love and promote her Puerto Rican identity and pushed people of color of many different nationalities to do the same for themselves.

During the 1960s, Rita continued to struggle finding work. Even after winning an Oscar, the only jobs that producers offered her were the same ones they had before, including Latina characters in gang movies. Rita vowed she would never accept those roles again.

In 1964, Rita boarded a ship named the *France* and moved to London. There, she began to act in the theater. She landed a part in the musical *She Loves Me* in the West End, London's version of Broadway, New York, where there are many theaters to choose from to see plays and musicals.

When she moved back to the United States later that same year, she decided to continue acting onstage and went to New York.

Lorraine Hansberry

She was cast as the female lead in a new Broadway play called *The Sign in Sidney Brustein's Window*. It was written by Lorraine Hansberry, who was the first African American woman to have a play produced on Broadway with *A Raisin in the Sun*. *The Sign in Sidney Brustein's Window* was the second play she had written. But Lorraine became very ill with cancer while the cast and crew were rehearsing. It ran for 101 performances. While

the play did not receive good reviews, it was an important stepping stone for Rita, not only for her budding career as a Broadway actress but also for finding love.

# CHAPTER 8
# Meeting Lenny

While Rita was working on Broadway, her friend Leah Schaefer asked her if she wanted to meet "the most wonderful man in the world" and introduced her to a doctor named Leonard "Lenny" Gordon.

Lenny Gordon

Rita liked how kind and funny Lenny was and said yes when he invited her to a New Year's Eve party. When Rita told him to meet her at Henry Miller's Theatre, where *The Sign in Sidney Brustein's Window* was being performed, he was confused as to why.

Lenny didn't realize he was going on a date with *the* Rita Moreno until he saw her name in the theater! They were married in 1965 and lived in New York City. Lenny Gordon was a well-known doctor who helped anyone who came into his office. It didn't matter where they were from, or if they were white or Black.

In 1966, when Rita was thirty-four years old, she gave birth to her only child, her daughter, Fernanda. She was so excited for her mother to meet her daughter but was disappointed when Rosa only talked about how hard she worked on knitting cute outfits for Fernanda. For Rita, it reminded her how she was raised to be a doll for her mother to show off. Rita vowed she would never treat Fernanda the same way. She would encourage her daughter to do what she wanted and would always support her and her dreams.

While Fernanda was still a toddler, Rita had a difficult time finding work.

She decided one day, in 1968, to call Marlon Brando, whom she had remained in contact with after their breakup years earlier. Marlon immediately offered her a role in his newest movie, *The Night of the Following Day*, which was based on a book called *The Snatchers*. It told the story of the daughter of a rich family being kidnapped.

It was sometimes difficult working with Marlon. It had taken Rita a long time to heal from their past relationship. It would be the last movie they were ever in together.

Rita managed to find a bit more work through the years, acting with Alan Arkin in *Popi*, then *Carnal Knowledge* with Jack Nicholson in 1971.

One day, Rita was watching a new children's show with Fernanda named *Sesame Street*, created by Jim Henson. Rita instantly fell in love with the show and begged Jim to let her be on it.

She didn't care that her agents warned her that changing her job to work on children's shows would affect her career. As always, Rita did what she wanted.

Thanks to Fernanda, Rita began a new phase in her acting career: children's television.

## Jim Henson (1936–1990)

Born in Greenville, Mississippi, Jim Henson was a puppeteer, animator, actor, and filmmaker who created comedy and educational shows for children. He was best known for creating the

Muppets, puppet characters that were originally intended for adult audiences in 1955. He founded Muppets, Inc., in 1958, which later became the Jim Henson Company.

Jim helped make puppets for the show *Sesame Street*, which debuted on November 10, 1969. There, he created characters like Cookie Monster, Big Bird, and many more. He then created and wrote *The Muppet Show*, which debuted in 1976, a comedy show that had special guests like Rita Moreno, Julie Andrews, Steve Martin, and more, who "performed" in front of a Muppet audience.

The Jim Henson Company later made puppets for and produced films like *Labyrinth*, *The Dark Crystal*, and many Muppet movies, including *The Muppets Take Manhattan*.

## CHAPTER 9
## *The Electric Company* and an EGOT

Rita immediately got to work, and from 1971 to 1977, she performed with actors like Morgan Freeman on a children's show that helped children learn how to read called *The Electric Company*. The music for the show helped her win a 1972 Grammy Award for Best Recording for Children. Her favorite part of the show was imitating Tina Turner, a famous singer, and teaching kids how to pronounce *un* in words like *unzip* and *unbutton*. Her catchphrase in the show was "Hey, you guys!" She even guest starred in *Mister Rogers' Neighborhood*, a children's show that taught the importance of kindness and patience.

In 1975, when Rita was forty-four years old,

HEY, YOU GUYS!

she played Googie Gomez in the Broadway show *The Ritz*, a play written by Terrence McNally. In the play, Googie Gomez dreamed of being a Broadway actress, even though she was a terrible singer. In fact, Terrence created Googie because Rita inspired him with her humor.

Rita loved playing Googie, and her love and talent for the role helped her win a Tony Award for Best Featured Actress. In her speech she said, "Rita Moreno is thrilled, but Rosa Dolores Alverio from Humacao, Puerto Rico, is UNDONE!" And in 1976, she played Googie again when they adapted the play into a movie.

In 1976, she starred in an episode of *The Muppet Show*, singing a song called "Fever!" with the Muppet named Animal, and did a dance inspired by the French tango, where the partners move swiftly together. Rita danced with her Muppet partner, tossing and throwing him around the stage. With her performance on *The Muppet Show*, Rita won her first Emmy, an awards show that celebrates achievements made in television, for supporting actress in a variety or music program.

By winning the Emmy, Rita became the first Latina to achieve the EGOT. She would win a second Emmy in 1978 for Outstanding Lead Actress in *The Rockford Files*.

## EGOT

The EGOT stands for the Emmy, Grammy, Oscar, and Tony awards. When someone wins all four of them, it means they achieved excellence working in television, music, film, and theater. To date, there are only twenty-one actors who have become EGOT winners. They include Whoopi Goldberg, Andrew Lloyd Webber, John Legend, Jennifer Hudson, Viola Davis, Elton John, and Robert Lopez, who has achieved EGOT status twice!

Robert Lopez

In the 1980s, Rita continued to act in movies and television shows such as *The Four Seasons*, with comedian Carol Burnett. She loved working with Carol, and they constantly laughed on the set of the movie. From 1982 to 1983, she was in a television series based on the movie *9 to 5*, which starred Dolly Parton, Lily Tomlin, and Jane Fonda. Rita also guest starred in popular shows like *The Golden Girls*, *Miami Vice*, *The Nanny*, and more.

But in the 1990s, Rita discovered a new challenge in her acting career: her age.

## CHAPTER 10
## Age Is Only a Number

Rita was close to sixty years old and was struggling to find work again. This time, not just because she was Puerto Rican, or a woman, but because she was getting older. It wasn't always easy for people in Hollywood to cast older actors. In 1990, Rita auditioned for a television show but was not hired because she looked *young* for her age! And when she went to a different audition, the only roles producers wanted to give her were those of stereotypical minor characters, like the Latin mother or grandmother of the main character. These were roles with barely any screen time. Rita struggled to find work that excited and challenged her as an actress.

Lenny was supportive, but he didn't really understand show business. But it was Lenny's idea for Rita to go on tour and perform cabaret, live shows in front of an audience in restaurants, ballrooms, and nightclubs.

Rita did a small tour with Lenny, who had retired from being a doctor and now worked as her manager. Fernanda even danced with her occasionally. But while Rita enjoyed singing and dancing and traveling across the United States, she didn't like performing if audiences were too busy having dinner to pay attention to the show. She was the opening act for people like George Burns, a comedian who worked on *The George Burns and Gracie Allen Show*, and Sammy Davis Jr., a singer known for songs such as "I've Gotta Be Me" and for performing with Frank Sinatra and Dean Martin. "I was so lucky, sharing the stage with George and Sammy and so many other great performers who were models of perseverance for me," she wrote in her memoir.

In 1993, Rita was honored to be invited to perform for President Bill Clinton's inauguration. She, along with other Broadway actors like Joel Grey and Carol Channing, sang "Make Way for Tomorrow: America Sings Through Its Broadway Musicals."

A year later, in 1994, she recorded the voice of Carmen Sandiego for the cartoon *Where on Earth Is Carmen Sandiego?* about an international thief that was based on a computer game.

The television show won a 1995 Daytime Emmy Award for Outstanding Animated Children's Program. That same year, Rita's name was added as a star on the Hollywood Walk of Fame!

Even though *Carmen Sandiego* was a popular show, Rita wondered if she would be able to continue to find work as she grew older.

## Carmen Sandiego

The TV shows *Where in the World Is Carmen Sandiego?* and *Where on Earth Is Carmen Sandiego?* were based on a video game series created in 1985 about a thief who stole treasures from all over the world. It is up to the players who work as agents for ACME Detective Agency to stop her. The video game series became popular in schools as a way to teach students about geography, history, math, art, and other subjects.

In 1991, the game became a children's television show where three contestants competed by answering questions to discover where in the world Carmen Sandiego was. The show was a mixture of live action, CGI, and animation. It won six Daytime Emmys and a Peabody Award. Its catchy theme song "Where in the World Is Carmen Sandiego?" was sung by Rockapella.

90
75

One day, she had dinner with a writer and producer named Tom Fontana, who said he had a role for her in his new television series called *Oz*, an adult show set in jail. Rita, he explained, would play a nun who tried to help the men who were sent there. From 1997 to 2003, Rita played Sister Peter Marie, winning the 1997 CableACE Award, an award honoring excellence in American cable television, for Actress in a Dramatic Series. She also won several ALMA Awards for best actress in a television series. *ALMA* stands for "American Latino Media Arts," honoring representation of the Latin community in entertainment.

By then, she was over seventy, but Rita showed no signs of slowing down.

# CHAPTER 11
# One Day at a Time

In 1996, Fernanda got married, and Rita and Lenny moved to Berkeley, California, to be closer to her daughter. Fernanda later had two sons, Justin and Cameron, who were born in July 1998 and July 2000. Sadly Rosa, Rita's mother, passed away in 1999. Rita often wished she could hug her mother one last time, feeling that all the time they spent together was not enough.

In the same year Cameron was born, Rita received the Library of Congress Living Legends Award. This award is given to those whose work greatly influences America's diverse culture. Also in 2000, HOLA, the Hispanic Organization of Latin Actors, an organization trying to grow the representation of the Latin community in entertainment and media, made the HOLA Rita Moreno Award for Excellence, celebrating performers who demonstrate exceptional skill and impact in their craft.

Four years later, she was awarded the Presidential Medal of Freedom by President George W. Bush. This is the highest civilian award given by the United States, and Rita was honored to receive it.

Rita continued to guest star in more shows like *Law & Order*, *George Lopez*, and *Ugly Betty*. In 2009, she was presented with the National Medal of Arts by President Barack Obama.

In 2010, Lenny died after a serious heart attack. Rita was heartbroken. But eventually, she felt a new sense of freedom. The next stage of her life had begun.

While performing in *Master Class* at the Berkeley Repertory Theatre in California, Rita met the producer and artistic director Tony Taccone. They became good friends, and Tony came up with the idea to cowrite a play with Rita about her life. It took several tries before Rita finally agreed. She was afraid that talking about her life would recall a lot of painful memories. But with Tony's help, she was able to perform *Rita Moreno: Life Without Makeup* in 2011. The play was a huge success. The show inspired her to write a book about her life. *Rita Moreno: A Memoir* was published in 2013. That same year, when she was eighty-two, she was awarded the Lifetime Achievement Award from the Screen Actors Guild in a ceremony that exclusively honors and celebrates actors. "Late in the first act of my career, I was recognized with an Oscar," she said. "Hopefully . . . it's early in the third act of my life."

Rita continued to work in film and television. She was cast in shows such as *Happily Divorced* and *Jane the Virgin* with fellow Puerto Rican actress Gina Rodriguez, and movies like *Rio 2* and *Six Dance Lessons in Six Weeks*.

In 2015, Rita Moreno was celebrated at the Kennedy Center Honors. President Barack Obama described her as “a leading lady of her era, a trailblazer with the courage to break through barriers and forge new paths.”

In her speech to Rita, Gina Rodriguez, said: "When you followed your dreams, Rita, you gave me the allowance to follow mine." And then she thanked her for inspiring her to fight for her dreams to be an actress and fight for what was right.

"She made miracles happen for the chance to perform for us," said Lin-Manuel Miranda, a Puerto Rican actor and songwriter, honoring her love of the arts and determination to be an actress and perform on the big screen.

That same year, Rita released her first all-Spanish album *Una Vez Más*, which means "one more time." Then in 2017, Rita became one of the lead actresses for a comedy series called *One Day at a Time*, a remake of the original show that came out in 1975. In it, she played Lydia Riera, a Cuban grandmother. She won best supporting actress at the Imagen Foundation Awards for her role. The Imagen Foundation honors Latin representation in film, television, and streaming media like Netflix and Hulu.

## Gina Rodriguez (1984–)

Gina Rodriguez is an actor of Puerto Rican descent who was born in Chicago, Illinois. She had

her television debut at the age of twenty in a 2004 episode of *Law & Order*. Since then Gina has worked on films such as *Filly Brown*, *Ferdinand*, and *Annihilation*.

She is best known for her role as Jane Villanueva in the comedy series *Jane the Virgin*, for which she won a 2015 best actress Golden Globe. She also worked with Rita on a 2019 animated reboot of *Carmen Sandiego*.

Gina owns the production company I Can and I Will, which promotes diverse cultures and stories on-screen.

*One Day at a Time* received critical acclaim for episodes that talked about experiencing discrimination for being Latin, mental health, and exploring identity within the LGBTQ+ community. It was nominated for four Primetime Emmy Awards, and Rita was nominated for a Critic's Choice Television Award four years in a row. The show was revered until it ended in 2020.

But it wasn't the end for Rita. In 2019, she had been selected to receive the Peabody Award for Career Achievement. (It's an award originally created to honor achievements in entertainment that promote a strong message on social issues, the environment, and the universal well-being of humanity.) At that time, the executive director of the Peabody, Jeffrey P. Jones, said, "We are delighted to celebrate her many contributions to entertainment and media, as well as her passion for children's programming and important social issues." He highlighted that Rita's career had broken barriers since her debut in Hollywood.

Director Steven Spielberg revived *West Side Story* (2021), and Rita worked alongside him as executive producer and played a supporting role. She also starred in the sports comedy *80 for Brady* with Jane Fonda, Sally Field, and Lily Tomlin. The movie was inspired by the true story of several widowed women who gathered to cheer on the New England Patriots during football season. Rita also worked in *Fast X*, the tenth movie in the *Fast & Furious* franchise, with Vin Diesel and Jason Momoa. In *X*, Rita played Abuelita Toretto, the grandmother of Vin Diesel's character, Dom. And in 2023, she starred in the television comedy *Lopez vs. Lopez* with comedian George Lopez.

Steven Spielberg and Rita Moreno

Rita still seems to have the same energy she did as a child to dance and sing and act. She continues to fight for human rights and for the arts, working with the Jackie Robinson Foundation providing scholarships to minorities to help further their education. She's also worked with the National Endowment for the Arts and was a commissioner for the President's White House Fellowships and a member of the President's Committee on the Arts and Humanities. And in

2024, there was a Barbie doll made in her honor! The beautiful doll was styled to match the dress she wore when she won the Oscar in 1962.

Early in her career, Rita struggled to get professional recognition and suffered discrimination. She saw a lack of opportunities for Puerto Rican actors and even began to question her own identity because she was forced to play the same role over and over again. But with her struggles came many victories. Rita's courage to stand up for herself and others continued to inspire people to be themselves, be proud of where they came from, and never lose sight of their dreams. In a video dedicated to Gina Rodriguez, Rita confesses she did not set out to be a role model. "I was merely a frightened Latina girl lost in the maze of Hollywood." She had no role models who looked like her, and the only way she knew how to survive was to be true to herself. And while it wasn't always easy, Rita does not regret where her dreams took her.

Rita looks back on her life in her own book, reflecting on her many accomplishments: the films and plays she performed, the awards she won, making her mother and her Puerto Rican culture proud, her life with Lenny, and her daughter and grandchildren. For Rita, there is still so much more to see and many more dreams to fulfill.

She wrote: "Here I am, healthy, happy beyond what one reasonably expects, fully able to remember and reflect, and equipped to dream. . . . My heart is full."

# Timeline of Rita Moreno's Life

| | |
|---|---|
| 1931 | Rosita Dolores Alverio is born in Humacao, Puerto Rico |
| 1936 | Moves to New York City with her mother, Rosa |
| 1945 | Has her Broadway debut in *Skydrift* |
| 1950 | Signs a seven-year contract with MGM; changes her name to Rita Moreno; movie debut in *So Young, So Bad* |
| 1961 | Plays Anita in *West Side Story* |
| 1962 | Wins the Academy Award for best supporting actress in *West Side Story* |
| 1965 | Marries Dr. Leonard Gordon |
| 1971 | Stars in *The Electric Company* children's show |
| 1972 | Wins a Grammy Award for *The Electric Company* soundtrack |
| 1975 | Wins a Tony Award for Best Featured Actress in *The Ritz* |
| 1977 | Wins an Emmy Award for *The Muppet Show*, becoming the first Latin actress to have an EGOT |
| 2009 | Awarded National Medal of Arts by President Barack Obama |
| 2011 | Performs her one-woman show, *Life Without Makeup* |
| 2017 | Plays Lydia Riera in *One Day at a Time* revival |
| 2019 | Awarded the Peabody Award |
| 2021 | Acts in and produces Steven Spielberg's *West Side Story* |

# Timeline of the World

| | |
|---|---|
| 1931 | Empire State Building is completed in New York City |
| 1936 | Spanish Civil War begins |
| 1945 | World War II ends |
| 1950 | Disney premieres the animated movie *Cinderella* |
| 1954 | First Burger King fast-food restaurant opens in Miami, Florida |
| 1961 | The Beatles make their debut at the Cavern Club in Liverpool |
| 1965 | President Lyndon B. Johnson signs the Voting Rights Act |
| 1971 | Mount Etna erupts in Sicily, Italy |
| 1975 | *Wheel of Fortune* television game show premieres in the United States |
| 1977 | The disc record "Sounds of Earth" is launched into space |
| 2000 | PlayStation 2 console is released in Japan |
| 2004 | American swimmer Michael Phelps wins his eighth medal at the Athens Olympics |
| 2017 | A total solar eclipse occurs, crossing the United States coast to coast, on August 21 |
| 2019 | USA women's soccer team wins the FIFA Women's World Cup for the fourth time |
| 2021 | June 19, known as Juneteenth, becomes a federal holiday |
| 2023 | A total solar eclipse occurs on April 20 |

# Bibliography


***Books for young readers**

"Artists We Love: Rita Moreno." **Straz Center**. October 19, 2021. https://blog.strazcenter.org/2021/10/19/artists-we-love-rita-moreno/.

*Denise, Anika Aldamuy, and Leo Espinosa. ***A Girl Named Rosita***. New York: HarperCollins, 2020.

Hernández, Arelis. "Transcript: Race in America: Breaking Barriers with Rita Moreno." ***Washington Post***. February 10, 2021. https://www.washingtonpost.com/washington-post-live/2021/02/10/transcript-race-america-breaking-barriers-with-rita-moreno/.

Martín, Lydia. "Rita Moreno Overcame Hispanic Stereotypes to Achieve Stardom." ***Miami Herald***. September 14, 2008. https://www.latinamericanstudies.org/puertorico/rita-moreno.htm.

Moreno, Rita. ***Rita Moreno: A Memoir***. New York: Celebra, 2013.

Riera, Mariem Pérez, dir. ***Rita Moreno: Just a Girl Who Decided to Go for It***. Netflix, 2021.

"Rita Moreno biography and timeline." **PBS**. September 28, 2021. https://www.pbs.org/wnet/americanmasters/rita-moreno-biography-and-timeline/18466/.

Ryzik, Melena. "Rita Moreno: Pathbreaker, Activist, and 'A Kick in the Pants.' " ***New York Times***. June 25, 2021. https://www.nytimes.com/2021/06/25/movies/rita-moreno-interview.html.